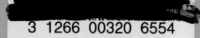

WHERE DO BABIES COME FROM?

WHERE DO BABIES COME FROM?

Written by Margaret Sheffield

Illustrated by Sheila Bewley

Alfred A. Knopf

New York   1974

THIS IS A BORZOI BOOK
PUBLISHED BY ALFRED A. KNOPF, INC.

Library of Congress Cataloging in Publication Data

Sheffield, Margaret.
    Where do babies come from?

    1. Sex instruction for children.   I. Bewley, Sheila,
illus.   II. Title.
HQ53.s53   1973   612.6'007   72–10044
ISBN 0–394–48482–7

Manufactured in the United States of America

Published April 30, 1973
Reprinted Three Times
Fifth Printing, September 1974

WHERE DO BABIES COME FROM?

Everybody in the world started life as a baby, like the baby in this picture which is drinking milk from one of its mother's breasts.

Everybody was a baby once, and every baby is made in the same way, by two grown-up people, a man and a woman—the baby's father and mother.

There is no way of coming into the world fully grown.

Babies begin life inside their mothers' bodies, in a special place called the womb.
You can't see the womb, because it is right inside the mother's body. But you can easily tell when a woman is going to have a baby because her whole belly looks bigger and rounder.
The woman in the picture is going to have a baby. She is pregnant.

If you could look inside the body of a pregnant woman, you would see the unborn baby curled up inside the womb where it is safe and warm and protected from the outside world.
The way out of the womb is through the vagina, which ends in an opening between the woman's legs. But the womb is kept tightly closed until the day the baby is ready to be born.

Young girls have a womb and a vagina, but they can't have babies until the womb is fully developed and their bodies are working like a grown-up woman's body.

Young girls also don't have any breasts or any hair under their arms or around the vagina. These things come as they grow up.

Boys are different from girls, of course.
Boys have a penis, which is joined to the body
between their legs. Under the penis there is
a small bag of skin with two small round-shaped
things inside. The name for these is testicles, although
because they're round like balls many people just
call them balls.

Men look like boys except that they're bigger and they have hair growing on various parts of their bodies.

Grown-up men have a special liquid in their testicles which comes out through the penis—not *urine,* which also comes out through the penis, but a special, different liquid with things called sperms in it. Sperms are invisible; you can only see them with a microscope.

A sperm is what makes a baby grow inside a woman.

Women have eggs in their bodies, tiny eggs about
the size of these dots..... They're kept right inside the
woman's body, near the womb.
To make a baby, a sperm from the man has to get to
one of these eggs in the woman.

The only way for the sperm to get to an egg is through the woman's vagina.

This is how babies are begun, with the man lying so close to the woman that his penis can fit into her vagina.

If one of his sperms can get to one of her eggs, a baby will begin to grow.

If a sperm manages to join up with an egg, they begin
to grow into a baby. But the egg is so small to begin
with that it takes three months to grow to the size
shown in the picture. It weighs about one ounce. It is
about two inches long.
But although it is so tiny, it is already beginning to
get the shape of a person, with a head and arms
and legs.

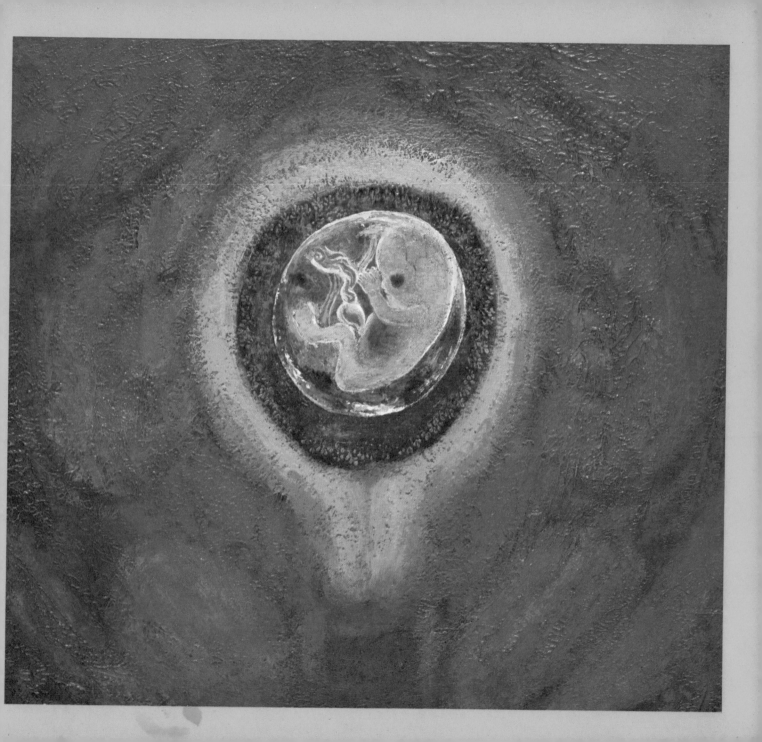

After the baby has been growing for six months it looks much more like a person. It can kick its feet and move its arms about. It has eyelashes and hair and fingernails. It has a heart that beats. It gets its food and oxygen carried to it by blood that passes through the cord joining the baby's body to the inside of the womb. You can see the cord in the picture.

After nine months inside the womb, the baby is ready to be born. It has everything a new baby should have. It's probably about twenty inches long and from five to ten pounds in weight. In the month before it is born it usually settles down low in the womb, upside-down, ready to come out.

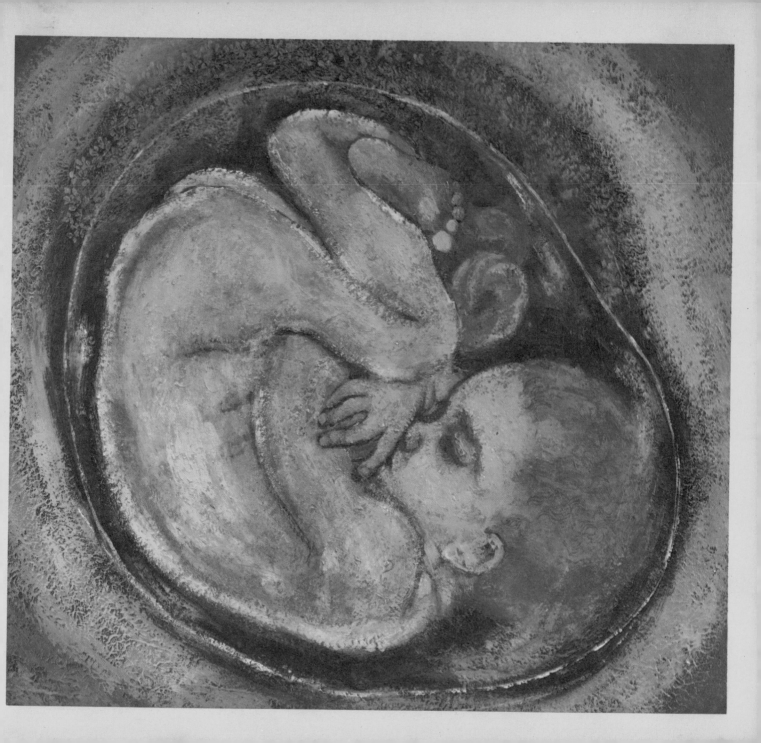

To be born the baby has to come out of the womb and down through the vagina. Mothers usually have a doctor or a nurse to help them with the birth, because it can take hours and hours, sometimes more than a day. The muscles that hold the womb tightly shut for nine months gradually relax and other muscles in the mother's body push the baby out.

When the baby is born it still has the cord that joined it to the inside of the womb. The nurse ties pieces of tape on the cord, to stop the blood coming out, and then cuts it, because it isn't needed any more. After this has happened the baby really is a separate person.

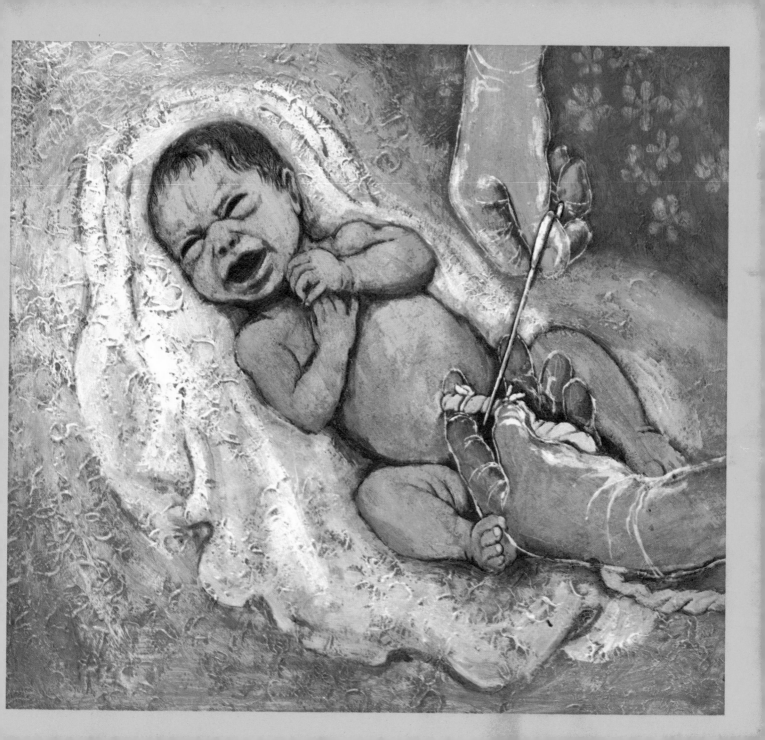

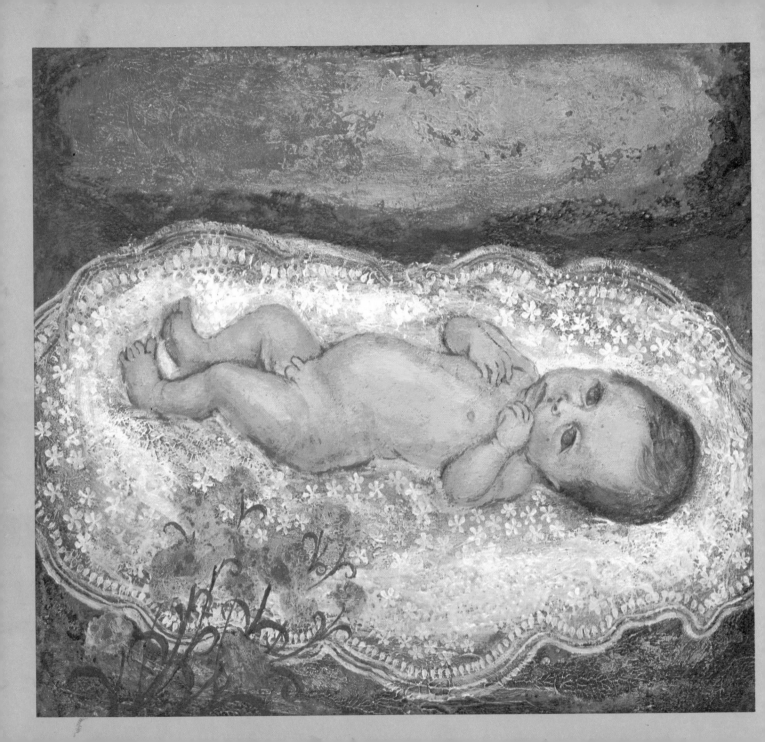

This is a boy baby. He has a penis. It's impossible to tell whether a baby is a boy or a girl while it is still in the womb. But as soon as it is born the doctor looks to see whether it has a penis or a vagina and immediately says to the mother, "It's a boy!" or "It's a girl!"

This is a girl baby. She has a vagina. Inside she has a tiny womb—and when she grows up she may have a baby herself.

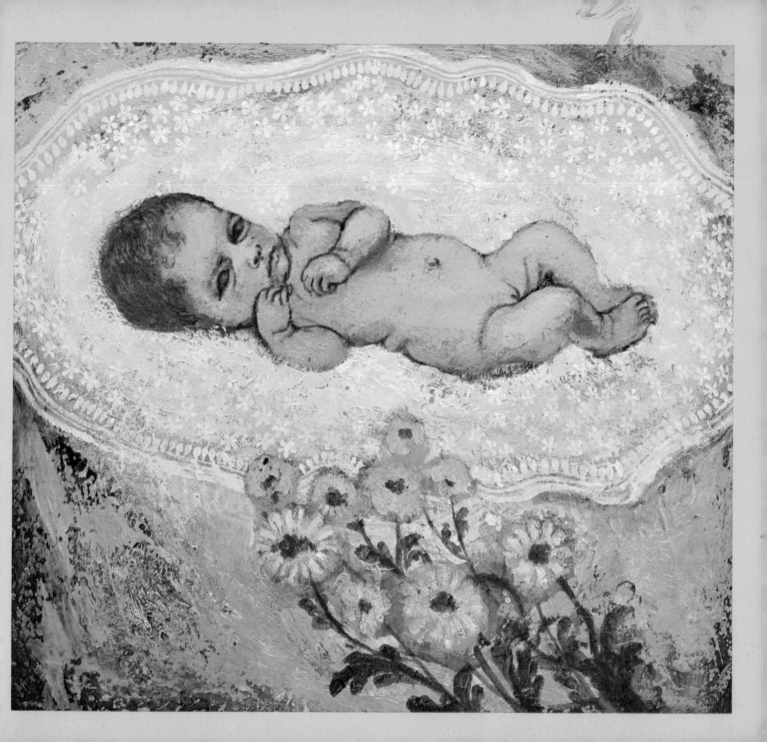

Everybody in the world started life as a baby and was made in the same way, by a man and a woman together. Everybody grew first inside his or her mother's womb and then was born.

And that's where babies come from.

ABOUT THE AUTHORS

Margaret Sheffield was born in 1940 in New Zealand, where she received a Science degree from the University of Otago. After teaching in New Zealand and London, she joined the BBC as a producer of School Radio programs. She is at present in Katmandu advising the government of Nepal on setting up school broadcasting there.

Sheila Bewley was born in 1939, studied illustration at St. Martin's School of Art in London, and did a year's post-graduate teaching in Bristol. After five more years of teaching, she became an artists' agent and a freelance illustrator. In 1967 she moved to Cornwall in southwest England. Her first child was born in the summer of 1968 shortly before she started work on *Where Do Babies Come From?*

A NOTE ON THE TYPE

This book was set on the Linotype in DeVinne, an
American type face that is actually a recutting by
Gustav Schroeder of French Elzevir. It was introduced
by the Central Type Foundry of St. Louis in 1889.
Named in honor of Theodore Low DeVinne, whose
nine-story plant called ''The Fortress'' was the first
building in New York City erected expressly for
printing, the type has a delicate quality obtained by
the contrast between the thick and thin parts of letters.
An enormously popular type during the early part
of this century, DeVinne combines easy readability
with a nostalgically atmospheric feeling.

Printed by Connecticut Printers, Inc.
Bloomfield, Conn. Bound by The Book Press, Inc.,
Brattleboro, Vt.
Typography and binding design by Virginia Tan